Tested over time, proven true by countless experiences, the solid foundations of excellence remain quality, service and teamwork. The stability of any organization depends on its willingness to build on this fundamental base.

QUALITY

Quality is never an accident; it is always the result of high intention, intelligent direction and skillful execution. It represents the wise choice of many alternatives. *Will A. Foster*

Life is no brief candle to me. It is a sort of splendid torch which I have got hold of for the moment, and I want to make it burn as brightly as possible before handing it on to future generations. *George Bernard Shaw*

The quality of a person's life is in direct proportion to their commitment to excellence, regardless of their chosen field of endeavor. *Vince Lombardi*

Thank God for competition. When our competitors upset our plans or outdo our designs, they open the infinite possibilities of our own work to us. *Gil Atkinson*

If it ain't broke – fix it. Take fast – make it faster. Take smart – make it brilliant. Take good – make it great. *Cigna Advertisement*

If you use your skill and imagination to see how much you can give for a dollar, instead of how little you can give for a dollar, you are bound to succeed.
Henry Ford

WELL DONE
IS BETTER THAN
WELL SAID. *Benjamin Franklin*

EVERYTHING SHOULD BE AS SIMPLE AS POSSIBLE, BUT NOT SIMPLER.

Albert Einstein

If things were done right only 99.9% of the time, we'd have two unsafe plane landings per day at O'Hare and 16,000 lost pieces of mail every hour by the U.S. Postal Service. Strive for 100% quality! *Jeff Dewar*

To lead a symphony, you must occasionally turn your back on the crowd.

It is just the little difference between the good and the best that makes the difference between the artist and the artisan. It is just the little touches after the average man would quit that make the master's fame. *Orison Swett Marden*

Reach beyond your grasp. Your goals should be grand enough to get the best of you. *Teilhard De Chardin*

Trifles make perfection, and perfection is no trifle.
Michelangelo

If a man is called to be a streetsweeper, he should sweep streets as Michelangelo painted, or Beethoven composed music, or Shakespeare wrote poetry. He should sweep streets so well that all the hosts of heaven and earth will pause to say, here lived a great streetsweeper who did his job well. *Martin Luther King Jr.*

The real friend of his country is the person who believes in excellence, seeks for it, fights for it, defends it and tries to produce it. *Morley Callaghan*

Quality is the daily pursuit of perfection.

Quality marks the search for an ideal after necessity has been satisfied and mere usefulness achieved.
Will A. Foster

The race for quality has no finish line.

PERFECTION IS OUR GOAL,
EXCELLENCE
WILL BE TOLERATED. *Jay Goltz*

QUALITY ONLY HAPPENS WHEN YOU CARE ENOUGH TO DO YOUR BEST.

Harold McClindon

Good is not good where better is expected. *Thomas Fuller*

People don't give a hoot about who made the original whatzit. They want to know who makes the best one. *Howard W. Newton*

If you haven't got the time to do it right, when will you find the time to do it over?

Many times the difference between failure and success is doing something nearly right...or doing it exactly right.

In business, the difference between winning and losing can be your commitment to doing a thousand little things right. Sweat the small stuff.

Quality products and quality service begin with quality thinking.

If you plant crab apples, don't count on harvesting golden delicious. *Bill Meyer*

Good enough is not 'good enough'.

No one ever attains very eminent success by simply doing what is required of him; it is the amount and excellence of what is over and above the required that determines the greatness of ultimate distinction.

Charles Kendal Adams

Good things happened when planned. Bad things happened on their own.

Don't settle for less, til better is best. *Gary Richard*

Hold yourself responsible for higher standards than anybody else expects of you. Never excuse yourself.

Henry Ward Beecher

IT IS A FUNNY THING ABOUT A BUSINESS, IF YOU REFUSE TO ACCEPT ANYTHING BUT THE BEST, YOU VERY OFTEN GET IT.

COUNTLESS, UNSEEN
DETAILS
ARE OFTEN THE ONLY DIFFERENCE
BETWEEN MEDIOCRE
AND MAGNIFICENT.

Quality does not come cascading like Niagara Falls...it comes one drop at a time.

When it comes to your product or project, people will take quality as seriously as you do, no more so.
Philip B. Crosby

Quality is the first thing seen, service is the first thing felt and price is the first thing forgotten. *Jay Goltz*

The road to quality is never smooth, but it's the only one that leads to long-term success.

Be quick but do not hurry. *John Wooden*

The price of success is hard work, dedication to the job at hand, and the determination that whether we win or lose, we have applied the best of ourselves to the task at hand. *Vince Lombardi*

SERVICE

Customers are not dependent on us, we are dependent on them. We are not doing them a favor by serving them, they are doing us a favor by giving us the opportunity to do so.

In business, there is only one boss...the customer. They can decide to fire everyone in the company, from the chairman on down...by spending their money somewhere else.

Every customer contact is a Moment of Truth. *Jan Carlson*

Customer service should flow smoothly, almost effortlessly. Everything about the business is touched and nourished by it. It's not a department, it's an attitude.

The road to greatness begins with making customer satisfaction an obsession.

Everyone smiles in the same language.

NEVER FORGET A CUSTOMER, AND NEVER LET A CUSTOMER FORGET YOU.

Harold McClindon

IT COSTS FIVE TIMES AS MUCH TO REPLACE A CUSTOMER AS IT DOES TO KEEP ONE.

Serve every customer with enthusiasm, compassion, competence. The competition may catch on, but they'll never catch up.

The polling place of any retail business is at the cash registers. Here, customer satisfaction can be easily measured in terms of both size and the frequency of the transactions. *Leonard Riggio*

There is only one way to build a business...satisfied customers, one at a time.

Our opinions aren't really relevant. It's only the customer expectations that matter. *Richard Notebaert*

Customer satisfaction can best be summed up in two words...exceed expectations.

When it comes to service put people first, paper second. *Leslie Charles*

Customer satisfaction, not customer service, is the mission.

To give real service you must add something which cannot be bought or measured with money, and that is sincerity and integrity. *Donald A. Adams*

Customer service does not come from a manual...it comes from the heart.

One of the most important principles of success is developing the habit of going the extra mile.

Napoleon Hill

LISTENING:

YOU CAN CONVEY NO GREATER

HONOR THAN

ACTUALLY HEARING WHAT SOMEONE

HAS TO SAY. *Philip Crosby*

BETTER THREE HOURS TOO SOON THAN ONE MINUTE TOO LATE.

Shakespeare

Customer satisfaction can energize the most positive advertising vehicle at our disposal...word of mouth.

Wayne Huizenga

A smile costs nothing, but when it comes to service... means everything.

Customer service is 80% attitude and 20% technique.

Leslie Charles

It takes months to find a customer; seconds to lose one.

The challenge is to not merely achieve 'customer satisfaction' but 'customer enthusiasm.'

To my customer: I may not have the answer, but I'll find it. I may not have the time, but I'll make it. I may not be the biggest, but I'll be the most committed to your success.

Consumers are statistics. Customers are people.

Stanley Marcus

Rule #1 – Use your good judgment in all situations. There will be no additional rules. *Nordstrom Employee Manual*

The only certain means of success is to render more and better services than is expected of you, no matter what your talk may be. *OG Mandino*

NOTHING IS EVER GAINED
BY WINNING
AN ARGUMENT AND
LOSING
A CUSTOMER. *C.F. Norton*

YOUR CUSTOMERS DON'T CARE HOW MUCH YOU KNOW UNTIL THEY KNOW HOW MUCH YOU CARE. *Gerhard Gschwandtner*

No business can make a profit manufacturing something unless the customer can profit by using it.

Sam Pettengil

Don't give the customer what they want, improve on it.

Think and feel yourself there! To achieve any aim in life, you need to project the end-result...Think of the elation, the satisfaction, the joy! Carrying the ecstatic feeling will bring the desired goal into view. *Grace Speare*

Goodwill is the one and only asset the competition cannot undersell or destroy. *Marshall Field*

My green thumb came only as a result of the mistakes I made while learning to see things from the plant's point of view. *H. Fred Ale*

TEAMWORK

Never doubt
that a small group of thought-
ful, committed people can
change the world; indeed it is
the only thing that ever has.

Margaret Mead

Many hands, hearts and minds generally contribute to anyone's notable achievement. *Walt Disney*

The secret is to work less as individuals and more as a team. As a coach, I play not my eleven best, but my best eleven. *Knute Rockne*

If I have been able to see farther than others, it is because I have stood on the shoulders of giants.

Sir Isaac Newton

Either we're pulling together or we're pulling apart.

For decades great athletic teams have harbored one simple secret that only a few select business teams have discovered, and it is this: to play and win together, you must practice together. *Lewis Edwards*

A HURRICANE:
MANY INDIVIDUAL RAINDROPS
COOPERATING.

NONE OF US
IS AS SMART AS
ALL OF US.

Ken Blanchard

Group desire is different than individual desire. With individual desire, it's up to you to feed the fire. With group desire, you get all kinds of people rolling logs on it from every direction. *Vince Pfaff*

No on can be the best at everything. But when all of us combine our talents, we can be the best at virtually anything. *Don Ward*

A company is known by the people it keeps.

No general can fight his battles alone. He must depend upon his lieutenants, and his success depends upon his ability to select the right man for the right place. *L. Ogden Armour*

Innovation is simply group intelligence having fun.
Michael Nolan

A team player tries to learn from those who are superior to him.

Winners can tell you where they are going, what they plan to do along the way and who will be sharing the adventure with them. *Dennis Waitley*

As a rule of thumb, involve everyone in everything.
Tom Peters

I've learned an important thing about living. I can do anything I think I can – but I can't do anything alone. No one can go it alone. Create your team!
Dr. Robert Schuller

There is no exercise better for the heart than reaching down and lifting people up. *John A. Holmes*

NO ONE CAN WHISTLE A SYMPHONY. IT TAKES AN ORCHESTRA TO PLAY IT.

H. E. Luccock

GIVE ALL THE CREDIT
AWAY.

John Wooden

The achievements of an organization are the result of the combined effort of each individual. *Vince Lombardi*

He has the right to criticize who has the heart to help. *Abraham Lincoln*

There is no higher religion than human service. To work for the common good is the greatest creed.
Albert Schweitzer

The best team doesn't win nearly as often as the team that gets along best. *Dr. Rob Gilbert*

Teamwork is the ability to work together toward a common vision. The ability to direct individual accomplishment toward organization objectives. It is the fuel that allows common people to attain uncommon results.

With geese, it is a fact that in the right formation the lifting power of many wings can achieve twice the distance of any bird flying alone.

Coming together is a beginning. Keeping together is progress. Working together is success. *Henry Ford*

All businesses can be reduced to three words: people, products, and profits. People come first.

When people with talent work together, expect a miracle. *Lee Iococca*

Anything one man can imagine other men can make real. *Jules Verne*

THERE IS NO LIMIT TO WHAT CAN BE ACCOMPLISHED IF IT DOESN'T MATTER WHO GETS THE CREDIT.

THE OBJECT IS NOT TO SEE THROUGH ONE ANOTHER, BUT TO SEE ONE ANOTHER THROUGH. *Peter Devries*

Snowflakes are one of Nature's most fragile things, but just look at what they can do when they stick together.

If people feel pride working for an organization, they will move mountains for its success.

Communication is the key that unlocks the door to teamwork.

Diversity: the art of thinking independently together.
Malcolm Forbes

If everyone is moving forward together, then the success takes care of itself. *Henry Ford*

The cost is low...
but the ideas are priceless!

Each title in the Successories "Power of One" library takes less than 30 minutes to read, but the wisdom they contain will last a lifetime. Take advantage of volume pricing as you share these insights with all the people who impact your career, your business, your life.

Anatomy of A Leader
This collection of insights by Carl Mays represents a thought-provoking body of knowledge that can help everyone develop the qualities of a leader. #713259

Attitude: Your Internal Compass
Denis Waitley and Boyd Matheson give powerful examples of how a slight shift in the way you see the world can yield powerful results in an ever-changing workplace. #713193

Companies Don't Succeed...People Do
Successories founder and Chairman, Mac Anderson, outlines "The Art of Recognition" – how to develop employees and a recognition culture within any organization. #716015

Rule #One
Author and customer service expert C. Leslie Charles has compiled dozens of insightful ideas, common sense tips and easy-to-apply rules in this customer service handbook. #716008

Dare to Soar
The spirit of eagles inspired this unique collection of motivational thoughts by Byrd Baggett. Any goal can be reached if you "Dare to Soar." #716006

Motivating Today's Employees
Recognition expert Bob Nelson offers a great primer on the impact of employee rewards and recognition. #716007

Motivation, Lombardi Style
Use the coach's memorable collection of insights about the athletic playing field and the business battlefield to inspire your team. #716013

Quality, Service, Teamwork
Share these 'foundations of excellence' with your employees to reinforce their importance in your organization. #716014

Teamwork
Noted consultant Glenn Parker gives managers, team leaders and members a valuable blueprint for successful team building. #716012